IMAGES OF ENGLAND

RETFORD
AND THE BASSETLAW AREA

View of Barnby Moor looking north, with the Old Bells Hotel in the distance. The hotel is one of the most distinctive in Nottinghamshire, and is set in several acres of grounds close to Sherwood Forest.

IMAGES OF ENGLAND

RETFORD
AND THE BASSETLAW AREA

PETER TUFFREY

The
History
Press

Retford's King Edward VI Grammar School First XI cricket team, 1951. The school was founded in 1552. The neo-Tudor red brick building with a central Gothic lantern and spire, by Decimus Burton, dates from 1855-57. A former boarding-house wing was extended in 1874, science rooms and gymnasium were added in 1896 and a new hall in 1937.

First published in 2003 by Tempus Publishing

Reprinted in 2009 by
The History Press Ltd
The Mill, Brimscombe Port,
Stroud, Gloucestershire, GL5 2QG
www.thehistorypress.co.uk

British Library Cataloguing in Publication Data.
A catalogue record for this book is available from the British Library.

ISBN 978 0 7524 2936 6

Typesetting and origination by
Tempus Publishing
Printed in Great Britain

Contents

Retford Town footballers walk on to the pitch at the start of the home game against Long Eaton United on 18 August 1961.

Introduction

Many of the pictures included in this book cover the first quarter of the twentieth century and show Retford as a small market town, which some will argue it still is today, as well as the surrounding Bassetlaw areas in their rural splendour.

A wide range of localities are included from all points of the compass: Scaftworth in the north, Carlton and Worksop in the west, South Leverton to the east and Bevercotes in the south.

The picture of Retford Market Place is a splendid view showing a typical market day with all sorts of characters, young and old, depicted. The one with the Town Hall in the back ground and seen on page 21 shows the encroach of the motor vehicle and maybe hints even in this view of the congestion it would subsequently cause.

For the Retford Cricket Club pictures, I was fortunate to meet well-liked local character and club secretary Mike Hall, who spent much time digging deep into the club's and his own personal archives to come up with a wide selection of images to choose from. One that is given pride of place of course is the one of Derek Randall, a good friend of Mike's and the club's who went on to perform wonders for county and country. I am indebted too to Richard Wharton who very patiently sorted out some rare action pictures featuring the Retford Football Club as well as some team pictures.

Perhaps what is a little surprising is the number of large and even medium-sized country houses that once existed in such a relatively small vicinity and played a major part in the running of the various areas and the lives of the people who once lived there. I am particularly fond of the pictures of Clumber House and think that it is a pity that the house is not still extant today and open to public view. This is because Clumber Park itself with all its various features is a major tourist attraction and has been for quite a number of years. The added attraction of a country house of this scale to view and walk round would have been more than an added bonus.

A variety of aspects of rural life are seen as we wonder round the Bassetlaw area, not least the number of hunt meets that are depicted, and it would have been very difficult to imagine at that time the amount of controversy this activity would cause in the ensuing years.

An example of how children once occupied themselves prior to television and other forms of electronic, digital and computerised entertainment is seen in the Hodsock Priory garden fête pictures. Another example of the more traditional forms of entertainment is the Boy Scouts picture at Gringley.

It is also interesting to note the number of pictures which include or are centred round the local post office, obviously fulfilling an important function at that time as well as providing communication with the big wide world beyond Retford and Bassetlaw.

The work of a few unidentified local photographers is featured but a large proportion of the pictures are from the camera of Doncaster-based photographer Edgar Leonard Scrivens, whose work I have used in a number of my publications.

Scrivens, according to his daughter Ivy who I spoke to during the mid-1980s, was born in 1883 obtaining his first camera when a schoolboy. Later, when Scrivens began producing postcard views, all bearing his initials E.L.S., he evolved a meticulous numbering system. For example on a card numbered 6-8, the first digit refers to the locality, in this case no. 6 relates to Retford. The second number denotes the postcard is the 8th in the Retford series. Scrivens photographed over 250 localities mainly in Yorkshire, Derbyshire and Nottinghamshire with a fair number of cards in each series.

In the 1920s and 1930s, he re-photographed a number of areas recorded earlier in his career, adding the letter 'G' or 'V' depending on the period, to the numbering on the cards. Scrivens also produced postcards of events, ranging from the Doncaster Aviation Meeting (Britian's first) in 1909 to the Misterton Hospital Procession.

When Scrivens died in 1950 and his business was sold, no one bothered to save the thousands of postcard-view negatives neatly filed in an upstairs room in his Doncaster business premises. Yet, his postcards, however, still exist and are a testament to his ability and achievement as a major topographical artist.

View of Blyth from the church tower.

One

Retford and Around

Bridgegate with Clarks Garage in the distance on the right. The layout of Retford has changed little since 1900, much of the street patterns having been established by that time. There has been a slow population increase in the area: between the 1831 census and the one taken in 1901 it grew from 5,999 to 12,340. During the following thirty years it reached 14,230. The growth in motor traffic was felt in Retford as much as anywhere else in the country.

Bridgegate seen from another direction, with Clarks Garage on the left. L.G. Wyse's North Road motorcycle and cycle depot and the Newcastle Arms public house are on the right. Wyse opened his business at No. 33 Bridgegate in 1892, but moved to another location in the street around 1906. The pub was the headquarters of the supporters of the Duke of Newcastle in the infamous election of 1826, where riots took place and troops were called in.

Bridgegate with the East Retford Electricity offices and showroom on the right. The Corporation began to supply the borough and most of the rural district with electricity in 1924. Five years later however, Retford and district was taking electricity from the Derbyshire and Nottinghamshire power company's sub-station at Checkerhouse. Retford's streets started to be lit by electricity from 1929.

Carolgate with the Picture House on the left. Retford once boasted four cinemas but, similar to other areas of the country, the town's interest in this form of entertainment has declined. *Son of India* was being shown when the picture was taken.

Carolgate. The Angel Inn can be seen on the left. Evans jewellers may be seen in the distance.

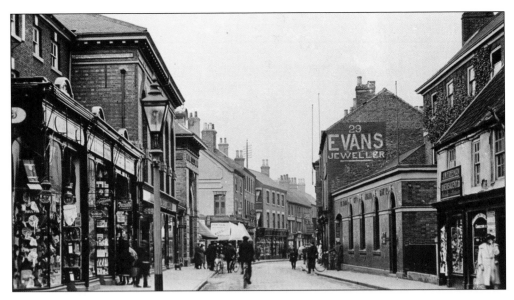

Carolgate once featured a number of well-known businesses including those of photographer Percy Laws, Yoell's jewellers, Evans jewellers (seen here), the Sheffield Union Bank and Fletcher's furnishing store. During the twentieth century a number of family businesses thrived in Retford, new ones were established and large multiples also took root there.

Market Square and Bridgegate featuring the White Hart Hotel on the left and a vehicle belonging to automobile engineers C. Clark & Son on the right, in front of Bolton's premises selling fish and poultry. The first licence for the White Hart – one of the best-known hotels in the district – was granted to William Riley in 1731. In 1828 it was noted that nineteen coach services stopped at the inn each day. This declined rapidly with the coming of the railways in 1849. The premises were enlarged in 1875. A sign on the White Hart notes that London is 144 miles away. It is also interesting to note that the town is 53 miles away from York, 26 miles from Sheffield, 36 north-east of Nottingham and 24 miles from Lincoln.

For much of Retford's history, the focal points and main areas of interest have been the town square and Market Place seen here. It was noted in *Kelly's Trade Directory* (1911) that 'The market, held every Saturday, is well attended and abundantly supplied with the produce of nearly thirty villages, large quantities being conveyed to Sheffield and other parts of Yorkshire. The chartered fairs are held on the 23rd March and 2nd October, for horses, cattle and cheese. There are also fairs held on the last Thursday in July for lambs, Thursday after June 11, and second Thursday in December, for cattle, sheep and horses. The Cattle Market is near the railway station; a market is held every Monday.'

Private houses along Holly Road, Retford. Until 1920 Retford had no council houses. Yet from this date the Corporation began building properties, some of the first being erected during phase one of the Hallcroft project. Further developments were seen in the first phase of the Ordsall estate and West Grove Road.

Market Square with the War Memorial on the left, bearing the names of 302 men who fell during the First World War. In 1945 a further 110 names were added. Retford's market once served the sizeable agricultural community and farm labourers would stand in the area waiting to be hired. The market square has since been pedestrianized and paved.

The Wesleyan chapel seen here on Grove Street, opened in 1880 on the site of a former building at a cost of £5,000. Four members of the congregation made substantial contributions towards this. The architects were Bellamy and Hardy, the designers of the Town Hall. Inside, an oval gallery and ceiling is like the one in the Town Hall. The building work was carried out by Thomas Hopkinson. It is an edifice of red brick and stone, in the Italian style and seated around 1,000. The inside features include an oval gallery, a rostrum and an ornate ceiling. Also attached to the building were vestries and a schoolroom.

View along London Road. Retford owed its Georgian prosperity to its position on the Great North Road, diverted through the area in 1766, and the Chesterfield Canal which opened in 1777. A little of this Georgian character remains, although most of the eighteenth and nineteenth-century houses are modest and altered.

View along Queen Street, Retford. In the Domesday Book, Retford was written 'Redeford'; early in the thirteenth century it was called 'Este Reddfurthe', and up to the middle of the nineteenth century it was known as 'East Redforde'. In AD 617 Retford was the scene of a battle between Edwin and Ethelred.

View along London Road, Retford. The types of clothes worn by the locals at this time can clearly be seen.

London Road, Retford, before the onslaught of the motor vehicle. The clear road may also suggest that heavy goods were being transported at this time on Retford's new railway network.

London Road, Retford, with two girls posing on the left. Photographer E.L.S. Scrivens always endeavoured to include children in his pictures whenever possible, to enliven the scene.

View along London Road. Whilst this may not be a particularly fascinating view, it reveals that Scrivens would take any picture if it was of interest to him, regardless of what others may think.

St Alban's church on London Road, Retford dates from 1901-03, and was designed by Hodgson Fowler. Pevsner states: 'Ashlar, Perp, with a large West window. Nave and aisles, but instead of a tower, a little spire on the North transept.'

The premises of Charles Lumley, decorator and furnisher. The business which subsequently included John Postlethwaite was established in Retford around the late 1890s, but was a short-lived venture. Maurice Stacey, a former director of the Doncaster furnishing company of Postlethwaite & Stacey was quoted in the *Doncaster Star* on 28 November 1991; '[The business] all started in Retford during 1897, when Charles Lumley a decorator, and John Postelthwaite established a furnishing business.' Two years later they opened a showroom in Doncaster's Oriental Chambers. 'John Postelwthaite had married my aunt Annie in 1890,' said Maurice Stacey, 'from what I can gather Mr Postelthwaite and Mr Lumley soon found that they could not get on together... this must have been discussed amongst the family and as a result, my father Arthur Stacey joined his brother-in-law in the firm around December 1900.'

Near to St Swithin's church is a
Russian cannon, which was captured
at Sebastopol during the Crimean war.
It was brought to Retford to celebrate
victory in the war.

Old cannon, Retford, with St Swithin's
church in the background.

Above and Opposite: Retford Town Hall was opened on 25 January 1868. It is a noble fabric with a domed roof, surmounted by an illuminated clock tower containing the clock formerly in the old town hall. The northern front, overlooking the market square is built of Bath stone, with plinths and columns of Red Mansfield stone, in the Romanesque style. The approach is by a vestibule, paved with encaustic tiles and thence by a grand staircase. At the top of the staircase there were three full-length portraits of James I and George II with his escort Queen Caroline, presented to the Corporation by Lord Monckton. At one time the building included a council room, Mayor's parlour and Record rooms, the former containing a marble bust of the Duke of Newcastle; under these rooms were the County Court offices. On the south side was the spacious hall with a gallery at the north end and at the south end a stage with retiring rooms; the large open space under the hall was occupied by the Butter and Poultry market.

On the canal at Retford.

Retford War Memorial, with the Wetsminster Bank on the left. 302 Retford men lost their lives during the First World War, and in 1921 a memorial was erected in the Market Place. Former Bassetlaw MP Sir Frederick Milner, unveiled it. After the Second World War, a further 110 names were added.

War Memorial, Retford. The town saw some enemy action during the First World War. On 2 September 1916 (a Saturday evening), German Zeppelins bombed the east side of Retford. Houses and gasometers suffered damage as a result.

Retford Motive Power depot, taken in the 1950s or '60s by well-known road and rail photographer Geoff Warnes from Doncaster.

The church of St Swithin, East Retford, is a cruciform building of stone in the late Perpendicular style, with traces of the Decorated period. It consists of chancel, with vestry, nave aisles, transepts, north chantry chapel, dedicated to the Holy Trinity and St Mary, south porch and a central embattled tower about ninety feet in height, with eight pinnacles. The chancel and tower fell down in 1651 and were subsequently rebuilt, and the chancel was further restored and enlarged in 1855, when an organ chamber was added on the south side. The reredos is of carved stone in the Decorated style. The central tower, thoroughly restored in 1855, is supported by four massive moulded arches of early English date. The church was completely restored under the direction of G.G. Place of Nottingham in 1855, when, in addition to the repairs already noted, the north aisle was taken down and rebuilt, and the external masonry of the nave, south aisle and transept renewed. The whole building was re-roofed and re-seated, the galleries being removed. In 1889 new choir stalls were erected and a year later, two new stalls for the clergy. In 1910 and 1914 the Corporation presented new stalls for its own use. There were 650 sittings, the register dating from 1573.

Right and below: Two views of the interior of East Retford church.

The post office at the Church Street/Town Street junction, South Leverton.

Barnby Moor, facing south along the Great North Road towards Kennel Drive. Shop Row is on the left and includes Dove Cottage and Pear Tree Cottage. Barnby Moor is three miles north west of Retford.

Looking north along the Great North Road near the junction with Old London Road. The White Horse Inn is on the left and at that time the premises were supplying Hewitt (the Grimsby brewers) golden medal ales and stout. Tom Bradley, in *The Old Coaching Days in Yorkshire* (1889) states: 'Not only from the Blue Bell were the Mails horsed in Mr Clark's time, but he likewise horsed coaches from another though a much inferior hostelry a little lower down the village. This house, which is still in existence and occupied as an inn, is known as the White Horse, and is the same to-day [a small, plain red-brick building with a red tiled roof] as it was in the old coaching days. Mr Clark used to stand his horses at the pretty extensive stabling at the back. There are those who can still remember the long rows of stables, the numerous paddocks crowded with young stock, and the extensive farm which supplied the stables with hay and corn.'

New kennels of the Fitzwilliam (Grove) hounds at Barnby Moor.

Looking north along the Great North Road with Ye Old Bells in the distance. The hotel has been known as The Bell Inn, and can be traced back to at least 1680. Throughout the eighteenth and early nineteenth centuries, the establishment was known as the Blue Bell.

View looking south-west along Old London Road, Barnby Moor. Glebe Farm is on the right. At one time the principal landowners at Barnby Moor were Col. Henry Denison CB and the Duke of Newcastle. The Rt. Hon. Francis John Savile Foljambe PC was lord of the manor.

Ye Olde Bells at Barnby Moor. Tom Bradley in *The Old Coaching Days in Yorkshire* (1889) mentions: 'This noted inn has undergone but little change since the time when the late George Clark ruled its destinies... The old stucco front has been replastered and painted, and the old archway leading into the spacious courtyard in the interior converted into a reception room. The four magnificent elms no longer rear their majestic heads. Two of them were blown down a few years back by a hurricane, and the remaining two were removed for fear of accident. The horse pond which formerly stood in front of the inn and stables has for many years been filled up, and a luxuriant shrubbery now marks the spot where the ablutions of coach and chaise were once performed.'

Meet of the Fitzwilliam (Grove) hounds at Barnby Moor, 19 April 1909, featuring the Duchess of Newcastle.

Meet of the Fitzwilliam (Grove) hounds at Barnby Moor, 19 April 1909.

Two

Retford Sport

Retford Cricket Club pavilion. Note the man, George Darwin, cutting the grass with help of a donkey, wearing 'special' footwear to avoid damaging the turf. The photograph dates from around 1915. Retford Cricket Club was formed in 1850. The club has enjoyed much success during the post-war years. The team won the Bassetlaw and District Cricket League Division One Section A championship in 1949, '68, '69, '76, '77, '78, '84 and '96 and were runners up in 1972 and 1993.

Retford Cricket Club's Second XI, 1949. Back row, from left to right: Des Wilson, George Noble, Ken Walker, Austin Glenn, Frank Smith, Bert Swift. Front row: Tommy Hopkinson, Horace Hoggard, Fred Stinchcombe (Snr), 'Coke' Charlton, A. Hopper, Ted Bellamy.

Retford Grammar School's First XI cricket team 1951. Back row, from left to right: Ron Widdowson, John Fishburne, Peter Pratt, David Gilbert, Trevor Lawless. Front row: Ted Waterford, Cordall, David Minitt, Peter Snell (captain), John Fawkes, M.J. Hall, -?- Shone.

Retford Grammar School's First XI cricket team, 1952.

A scene from a Retford Cricket Club annual dinner held at the Pheasant Hotel during the 1960s. Those depicted include Ken Brambrook, wicket keeper; Alan Wilkinson, spin bowler; Geoff Ostrick, President; Nobby Clark, captain and Ken Wilkes (the only player present in two Retford successes; the League in 1949 and promotion into section A 1954).

Peter Hacker in action for Retford Cricket Club in a match against Welbeck in 1975. Peter is described as one of Retford Cricket Club's foremost players in the post-war years. He went on to play for Nottinghamshire and gain his County Cap.

Derek Randall was born in 1951 and played for Retford Cricket Club from the age of nine. He made seven centuries during his career with England, the most spectacular being the 174 he scored against Australia in the Centenary Test in Melbourne. On returning to England a civic reception was held for him at Retford Town Hall. The signed souvenir picture reproduced here was one of many made to satisfy requests that were made for his autograph.

Retford Cricket Club's First X1, 1968. Back row, from left to right: Stephen Birkett, David Haw, Derek Randall, Derek Armstrong, John Brown, Jim Harkin, Keith Jackson. Front row: Colin Loates, Geoff Key, Alan Bull, Mike Hall, Fred Self, John Coddington. In 1968 the team won the Bassetlaw and District Cricket League Division One Section A championship.

In September 1978 the Retford Cricket Club pavilion was destroyed following an attack by vandals. Derek Randall is pictured here near the ruins of the building. Over the ensuing weeks, he lent a helping hand by fronting a campaign to raise funds for a new pavilion.

Opposite below: On 1 May 1994, Retford Town Cricket Club played a match against the stars of the television soap *Emmerdale Farm*. This was to celebrate the opening of the club's new practice pitches. Those pictured include Chris Hall, Mike Quigley, Derek Underwood, Fraser Hines, Peter Trend, Simon Hempsall and Brian Wilson.

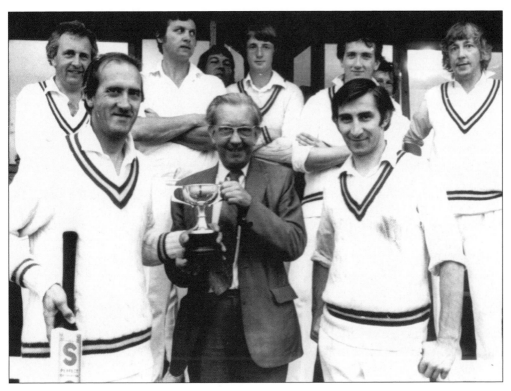

Scene at a Worksop versus Retford Town cricket match in 1980. Harry Bartlett of the *Worksop and Retford Guardian* is seen presenting the 'Twin Town Trophy' to man-of-the-match M.J. Hall, who scored 83 not out. Others in the picture include Geoff Key, Alan Bull, Chris Hall, Nigel Hall, Derek Armstrong, Tim Jones, Keith Jackson and Alan Old.

Retford Town Football Club team group photograph. Retford Town was formed in 1949 and they joined the Yorkshire League Division 2. Their honours included Champions of Division 2 and they were promoted to Division 1, being champions of Division 1 (1958/59). In 1961 they joined the Midland League, the Derbyshire Premier League in 1980 and Northern Counties (East) League 1983. In 1983/84 they were champions of Division 2 south. In 1985 they withdrew from the League through mounting debts.

Opposite above: Retford Cricket Club, 12 May 2001. Back row, from left to right: Steve Walker, Pascal Broadley, Dave Savage, Mike Hall (secretary), Brian Woods, Jamie Hart, Eddie Boyes. Front row: Andy Duckering (scorer), Ben Thorpe, Stuart Adams, Mike Waterfield, Nigel Hall (captain), Steve Musgrove.

Opposite below: Retford Town, Yorkshire League champions 1958/59 season. Back row, from left to right: J. Shillito, D.M. Rodgers, A. Brown, C. Wooliscroft. Centre row: R. Shaw, B. Topham (secretary), G. Rogerson, J. Harrison, R. Wharton, E. Barkworth (trainer), C.H. Walker (manager). Front row: H. Hardy, D. Holmes, J. Hall, T. Haydon, P. Bradley.

Action during the Yorkshire League game between Retford Town and Frickley Athletic, on 27 August 1959. Retford lost the match 3-0.

Retford Town line up before the start of a game.

Retford Town FC celebrate their cup victory.

A scene from a match in around 1972 where Sir Frederick Milner's School First XI played against a side made up of staff. Chris Hall is one of the players identified.

Three

Around Worksop and Clumber

Worksop cricket team pose for the camera.

Bridge Street, Worksop. The history of the small town may be traced back to Anglo-Saxon times.

Market Place, Worksop, the area has seen much redevelopment during the intervening years, the properties on the right being cleared in the post-war years. The Lion Hotel is the only surviving hostelry in the picture, the Royal Hotel having closed some time ago.

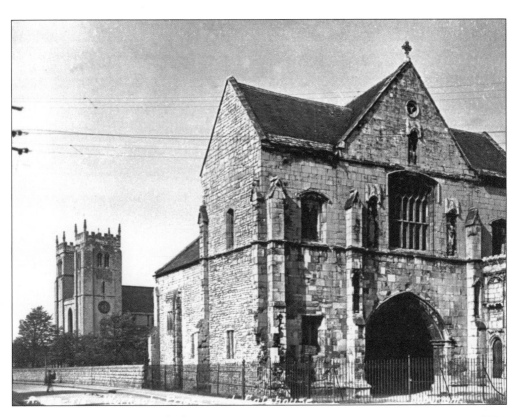

Worksop Priory gatehouse, which is generally felt to be one of the most interesting buildings in the county. Its features include a pre-Reformation statuary and a unique projecting wayside shrine to accommodate an image of Christ. On the left is the Augustinian Priory of St Cuthbert and St Mary.

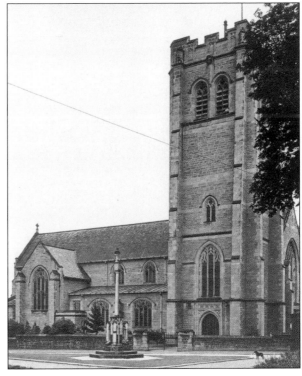

St Anne's church and war memorial.

This picture shows a scene at Grange Farm, Bevercotes, south west of Worksop, around 1914.

Earlier houses had existed at Thoresby before the one shown here was erected. It was, according to Pevsner, 'far more ambitious than any other of the Victorian age in the county and a lasting monument to the self-confidence of at least one section of the nineteenth century nobility... The main fronts are on the south and east, 182 and 180 ft long respectively... The main staircase rises in a series of double flights under the central tower. The third Earl Manvers commissioned the building from Anthony Salvin who was the master of early and mid-Victorian neo-Tudor design in England. The style of the interior is mainly Jacobean with some eighteenth-century reception rooms.

Deer in Thoresby Park.

Welbeck Abbey, east front.

The bird room at Welbeck Abbey

Welbeck Abbey is a considerable structure in varied styles of architecture. The south front, of three storeys, has two boldly projecting square towers. The east front, overlooking the lake, rises from a broad terrace with a double flight of steps to the lawns below and exhibits a series of Tudoresque gables, agreeably breaking the long line of the roof. The west front is in a semi-castellated style and includes a large square embattled tower. It has been recorded that 'the late Duke [of Portland] who died 6 December 1879, had held possession of the estate since 1854, and during that period, while living almost wholly in retirement, expanded vast sums of money in laying out the grounds, erecting farm buildings and lodges and in constructing those subterranean apartments and corridors which have rendered Welbeck at once unique and famous... the interior of the mansion contains a large Gothic hall restored in 1751, and remarkable for its fan-traceried ceiling and elaborate decorations. Of the many buildings outside the abbey the most remarkable is the riding school, an immense structure nearly 400 feet in length... the extensive park, portion of Sherwood Forest, abounds with deer and contains several specimens of forest trees... the lakes include several fine sheets of water upwards of four miles in length.'

Welbeck Abbey, south front.

Welbeck Abbey from the gardens.

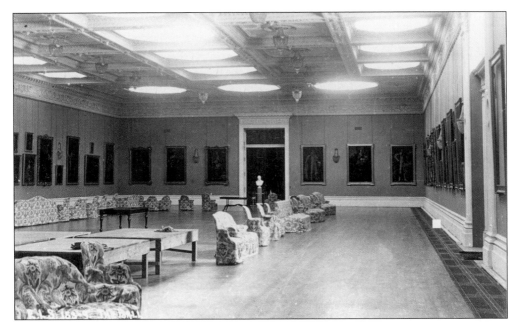

In 1916 it was mentioned that the ballroom at Welbeck Abbey 'is 170 feet in length by about 70 wide. The roof is supported by massive iron girders, and the room is lighted in the daytime by 27 octagonal lights and at night by splendid crystal chandeliers. It has an extremely fine oak floor and is now used as a picture gallery, the collection hung here comprising about 160 grand works by ancient and modern masters.'

The Lion Gates at Welbeck Abbey.

The Clumber estate formed part of Sherwood Forest until 1707 when licence was given to John Holles, the third Duke of Newcastle, to enclose it as a Park for the Queen's use. Clumber House was built in around 1760-70 by Stephen Wright for the Duke of Newcastle. The basic layout included four wings around a central block. Clumber Bridge, seen in one of the pictures, was built about 1770 to the designs of Stephen Wright consisting of three almost semi-circular arches. A large serpentine lake was constructed at a cost of over £6,000 between 1774 and 1789. Plans for alterations to the House were made in 1814, 1829 and 1856 by architects Benjamin Wyatt, Sidney Smirke and Sir Charles Barry. In the event, only Smirke's designs, with an Italianate flavour, were carried out. However, in the late 1870s, fire damage caused the central part of the house to be rebuilt in the Italianate style to the designs of Charles Barry, the younger. A private chapel for the Duke of Newcastle's use, Gothic in style, containing stained-glass windows by Kempe and dedicated to St Mary, was erected in 1889. The House existed until 1937, when the ninth Duke raized the house and lakeside terraces to the ground.

During the Second World War, Clumber Park was used as a munitions dump. In 1946, the Park was sold by the Duke to the National Trust, now English Heritage. People presently visit the Park for the peace and freedom, which they find there.

Whilst Clumber House was demolished in the late 1930s, there still remains, intact, some interesting features within the Park. These include the Entrance Gates, built in 1789, off the Worksop Road; Carburton Lodge; the Drayton and Normanton Gates; Apley Head Lodges and Gate; two eighteenth-century Doric Temples designed by Stephen Wright; the Duke's Study set back from the main house site; eighteenth and nineteenth-century stables.

The bridge at Clumber.

The grounds of Clumber House, showing the *Lincoln*.

Four

Carlton and Hodsock

Entrance to Carlton Hall, Carlton-in-Lindrick.

Carlton Hall, dating from the late eighteenth century, was built by Mr Ramsden of the Carlton family. It replaced a hunting lodge built in the early seventeenth century. During the early twentieth century the hall was the property of Charles Plumptre Ramsden who was also the lord of the manor and the principal landowner. The hall was described as a large and handsome mansion in the Classic style with beautiful grounds. Carlton Hall has since been demolished.

Another view of Carlton Hall.

The Green, North Carlton.

Garden fête at Hodsock Priory, 8 July 1909. The *Doncaster Chronicle* of 16 July 1909 reporting on the Hodsock Priory event included the following in its report: 'In the glorious weather of Thursday [8th July] , a children's fête was held at Hodsock Priory, in aid of the Blyth and District Nursing Association, in which the Misses Mellish take so great an interest. The fête commenced with a Kinderspeil (German for children's play), bringing in a number of Nursery Rhymes. The subtitle was old friends with new faces. As soon as the gong was sounded a pretty little fairy (Edith Booth) with a silver wand, in a snowy dress, and wearing a crown of silver tinsel, entered and invited the children to gather for play, and while the elder ones sang very sweetly some appropriate choruses... Maypole dances followed, given by 24 girls of the Upper School (mixed), and was very cleverly done, and there was some very pretty singing. The entertainment concluded with a procession through the grounds of infants, Maypole children, dressed in pink and white alternatively, and 36 other boys and girls dressed in the national costumes of England, Scotland and Ireland, and two little boys dressed in khaki, carrying Union Jacks, headed the procession. Patriotic songs were sung at the finish, under the guidance of the headmaster, Mr Spencer. There were two performances and three and six o'clock. Miss F. Grocock conducted the Maypole dances, and Mrs Steele presided at the piano. Pask's (Worksop) Band was in attendance, and accompanied the Maypole dances and patriotic songs, and later played for dancing in the evening. The attendance was remarkably good at both performances. Most of the gentlemen's houses in the neighbourhood were represented in the afternoon.'

Children in fancy-dress costume at the Hodsock Priory garden fête on 8 July 1909.

Children in fancy-dress costume at the Hodsock Priory garden fête on 8 July 1909.

Opposite below: Hodsock Priory, at one time the seat of Henry Mellish Esq. DL JP, is a mansion of red brick in the Elizabethan style, and once described as being 'pleasantly seated amid gardens and pleasure grounds'. Henry Mellish was lord of the manor of Hodsock and the former principal landowners in the area were Mellish himself and the Right Hon. Francis John Savile Foljambe, Edward Charles Riddell, Sir Archibald Woollaston White and Sydney Gladwyn Jebb.

Hodsock Priory is really a fictitious name as there was actually no priory here. There was a large moated manor house, dating from around 1250-53, that belonged to the Clifton family at the time that a gatehouse was built, which according to Pevsner is the only feature in the area from the early sixteenth century. He also notes, 'The house lies at right angles to the gatehouse. The oldest part, facing south-west, looks as if it is early nineteenth century... The exterior was remodelled by Devey in 1873-76 for Mrs Mellish, who filled in the segmental window heads with brick-nogging and added corbelling as on the gatehouse.'

A view of Hodsock Priory.

Five

Blyth, Oldcotes and Ordsall

Nornay, a hamlet situated north of Blyth, was formerly a farming community comprising several large houses, farmhouses and buildings. Looking towards the A1 (skirting the village), the building on the right has since been demolished. Nornay Farm cottage is to the left.

Facing the village with Nornay House on the right.

Blyth, ancient name 'Blia', has been described as an extensive parish and township, seated on the River Ryton. Blyth once had a market, and was on the high road from London to York. However, many years ago the market was removed to Bawtry. N. Pevsner in *Buildings of England; Nottinghamshire* says 'the village is really a decayed market town which grew up outside the gates of the abbey, important to medieval travellers.' In this picture Archway House can be seen in the centre.

Angel Inn, with Bawtry Road on the left leading out of the village. Records relating to the Angel Inn are said to extend back to the late thirteenth century. At the time the picture was taken John Armstrong was the landlord at the Angel.

A bird's eye view of the village from the church tower. The Church of SS Mary and Martin, standing on an elevated site, is a stone building mostly of Norman date, with later additions, consisting of chancel, nave, aisles, south porch and a fine embattled western tower, with pinnacles at the angles, containing a clock and six bells, recast around 1841. The south aisle has a screen separating it from the chancel. There are memorial windows to Mrs Sewel, General Simpson and Mrs Walker, erected by Mrs Weldon, and a number to the Mellish family.

Blyth Hall from the lake. 'A handsome mansion of brick with stone dressings, in the Tudor style, surrounded by well-wooded pleasure grounds and commanding extensive views.' At the time the picture was taken – around 1916 – the hall was the seat of Major Francis Willey JP, who was also lord of the manor.

Street scene at Blyth with the church in the distance. At the east end of the nave, which has a stone groined roof in the Early Pointed style and formed part of the ancient priory church, are the remains of a wall painting from the fifteenth century. The church was restored in 1885 at a cost of £3,544, and once afforded 400 sittings. The register dates from 1556.

High Street, Blyth. The population during the first decade of the twentieth century was around 640.

High Street, looking back to the church with Lichfield House on the left.

Blyth Wesleyan Methodist chapel, which carries a stone bearing the date 1902.

Blyth, with the Fourways hotel in the distance. Blyth was once an important stopping place for coaches, being on one of the old roads from London.

A street scene at Blyth. At one time, fairs for horses and cattle were held on Holy Thursday and 20 October.

View of the Green and church in the distance. The church of SS Mary and Martin, standing on an elevated site, is a stone building mostly of Norman date, with later additions, consisting of chancel, nave, aisles, south porch and a fine embattled western tower, with pinnacles at the angles. The church was restored in 1885 at a cost of £3,544 and at one time could seat 400. The register dates from 1556.

A street scene at Blyth with the Red Hart Hotel to the left. During the early part of the twentieth century, the residents' occupations included a basket maker, shoemaker, pork butcher, wheelwright, farmer, blacksmith and grocer.

The Memorial Hall, Blyth.

View featuring the White Swan public house on the right. One of the noted landlords at the pub was John Eastland.

Blyth donkey race.

A view from near the church looking towards the Red Hart (on the left) and the Fourways public house at the centre of the picture.

View along Spital Road.

Blyth Rose Cottage. Note the attractive window designs.

A view of Blyth schools.

Street scene at Oldcoates, with a postman posing for the camera. The area known as Styrrup-with-Oldcotes (or Alcoates) formed a township, partly in the parish of Blyth, but largely in that of Harworth.

38-1. ROMAN CATHOLIC CHURCH, OLDCOATES.

The Roman Catholic church of St Helen on Main Street, Oldcotes. It dates from around 1869-71 and was designed by S.J. Nicholl.

Street Scene at Oldcoates with W.C. Hill's premises on the left. The population in 1911 with Styrrup was 501. Viscount Galway was a former lord of the manor, and the trustees of Shrewsbury Hospital were the principle landowners.

A view of Ordsall, near Retford.

Six

Harworth and Bircotes

Harworth is situated on the Nottinghamshire/Yorkshire border, and until the sinking of the colliery, was a small agricultural village. The venture was the brainchild of a Leeds University professor and initially the project was funded by a group of German financiers. The picture above features the drapery business of Revill & Marshall.

Waterstock Road, Harworth.

Sinking at Harworth Colliery was started by a Leeds University professor during the early twentieth century. He used German money and labour to sink the shafts until the operation was halted by the intervention of the First World War, which saw the foreigners interned. However, the work was later resumed and completed during the early 1920s.

Harworth Colliery was bought by RJB in 1994 and the company still own it today. The pit has recently undergone heavy investment in deepening the shafts and upgrading its winders. The current manpower employed is around 600.

Gilbert Road, Bircotes.

Scrooby Road, Bircotes. On the right is Droversdale Road. Harworth Colliery is out of view to the left.

Harworth Miners' Welfare and Institute, off Swinnow Road, Bircotes.

Seven

Scrooby

Chapel Lane, Scrooby, with the old vicarage, probably dating from the late sixteenth century in the distance. Woofendon House is on the left along with the Methodist chapel, a brick-built and stuccoed structure with a hip-gabled slate roof, erected in 1829.

Scrooby is a parish and village on the Great North Road, which once boasted a station on the main line of the Great Northern Railway. It is eight miles north-west of Retford. Pilgrim Father William Brewster, who was the son of William Brewster Senior, lived for a time at Scrooby Manor House. The latter gentleman was bailiff of the Archbishop of York's estate at Scrooby from 1575-1590 and Master of the Queen's Postes.

A view of Scrooby.

Dog Lane, Scrooby, with the Green Man cottage on the left. The population of Scrooby in 1911 was 243.

References to St Wilfred's church at Scrooby, dedicated to an early Archbishop of York, can be traced back to around 1177. It has been described as an ancient embattled building of stone in the Early English and Decorated styles with a tower, surmounted by four pinnacles and a lofty octagonal spire and containing three bells, dated 1695. Pevsner states that 'the steeple has one unusual feature: the transition from the square to the octagonal spire.' In 1817 the spire was struck by lightening and suffered considerable damage and was struck again fourteen years later. The church underwent restoration in 1862 by public subscription. The register dates from 1695 and around the time the picture was taken the principal landowner was Viscount Galway.

A view of Scrooby from a distance taken by well-known local photographer Edgar Leonard Scrivens.

The original Scrooby Manor House, also noted as the Archbishop's Palace, was probably built in the twelfth century. The manor house would have been well situated as a hunting lodge, being close to the Hatfield Chace and Sherwood borders. By the early seventeenth century William Brewster Junior was holding meetings of the Scrooby Separatist Church there.

Having been allowed to fall into disrepair by the mid-seventeenth century, 'the dilapidated manor house and its outbuildings were demolished following a demolition order granted by Charles I', according to Malcolm Dolby in his book *Scrooby* (1991). He also adds that part of one wing of the manor house survived, and in around 1750 was renovated as a farm house for the Archbishop's tenant. It is that building which can be seen today.

Manor Road, Scrooby, with Low Farm and Palace Farm on the left and Alpha House in the distance. Dolby *op. cit* states: 'This imposing late eighteenth century three-bay brick farmhouse faces south overlooking the Croft... the farm was once part of the Scrooby Estate of the Viscounts Galway, and when the 8th Viscount attempted to sell the farm in 1931 it was advertised as being a good sheep and potato farm with an area in excess of 207 acres. The house is now a private residence.'

Entrance to Scrooby.

Wolsey Mill and ford spanning the River Ryton at Scrooby. The mill has since been converted into a private dwelling.

Low Road, Scrooby, looking north with Greenfield House and Teasel Cottage on the right.

Eight

Drakeholes
and Everton

Drakeholes is situated on the Gainsborough Road near Wiseton. It is also one mile south-east of Everton. The picture here shows the lodges at the original entrance to Wisteon Hall.

The Swan Inn at Drakeholes. The premises have since been renamed The Griff Inn.

The Inn is situated at a road junction and is adjacent to the Chesterfield Canal.

Looking along High Street with the village hall to the left. Northfield House is in the distance. There is currently an annual parish meeting held at the village hall each May.

The Sun Inn (selling Whitworth, Son and Nephew Ales) on the Gainsborough Road with Davenport House to the right. Mattersey Road runs between the two buildings. Everton is partly bounded on the east by the Chesterfield Canal and on the south, west and north by the River Idle. The former principle landowners included the governers of the Magnus Foundation, Clarkson's trustees, A. Smith Denton Esq. and Messrs Lonsdale.

Brewery Lane with Cobble Yard in the distance. Much redevelopment has taken place along the thoroughfare in the intervening years. The picture is another example of photographer E.L. Scrivens using posing children to add interest to a scene.

Old Post Office Street with Church Street in the distance. The parish of Everton falls within the Everton Ward of the District of Bassetlaw and the Misterton Electoral Division of the County of Nottinghamshire. The parish council's administrative area covers Everton, Harwell and part of Drakeholes.

Another view of the Sun Inn on Gainsborough Road. A fomer landord of the inn was Fred Lundy. At the time the picture was taken, Whitworths owned the pub. It is also interesting to note that the brewers are listed as having stores at Everton.

Bawtry Road where the Sun Inn can be seen in the distance. Everton's residents once ranged from a large number of farmers to a miller, and from a bricklayer to a surgeon.

Village scene at Everton, the area being situated on the Gainsborough to Bawtry Road.

Church Street with Church Farm to the right. At one time it was also called Old Carriage House. The church of the Holy Trinity is an ancient embattled structure, principally of the twelfth century, with some later work.

Above and below: The meet of the Fitzwilliam (Grove) hounds at Everton on 30 January 1911. Glebe Farm House is in the background of the picture below.

L.S.S. Meet Of The Fitzwilliam (Grove) Hounds At Everton, Jan. 30. 1911.

Gainsborough Road, looking south with the old post office to the left. A former sub post mistress was Mrs Ada Bowns. At one time, letters arrived from Bawtry at 7.55 a.m., and were dispatched at 9.55 a.m. and 6.40 p.m. There were no deliveries on Sundays.

Everton Wesleyan Methodist chapel on Chapel Lane. The building carries a date stone inscribed 1872.

Nine

Mattersey, Wiseton and Clayworth

View along Ranskill Road, Mattersey, the area being situated on the River Idle. The chapel, to the right at the junction with Job Lane, has since been converted into a private dwelling.

The pictures show the remains of the Gilbertine Priory of St Helen at Mattersey. It was founded there by Thomas Maresey before 1192. It stood about a mile from the present village and traces of it still remain. At its dissolution there were six canons and revenues valued at £55.

Mattersey Priory.

Opposite below: Mattersey Thorpe, near Thorpe Road. The properties on the left include the Gables, Bleak House Farm, the Poplars and Granary Cottage.

Mattersey bridge and church of St John the Baptist. The latter is an embattled building of stone, consisting of chancel, nave, aisles, south porch and western tower with crocketed pinnacles. In 1882 the gallery and organ were removed and the church restored at a cost of £110 and a further restoration was undertaken in 1886 and the tower arch opened out, at a cost of £400. The stained east window was inserted by the daughters of the late Revd W. Thorpe, a former vicar, at their own expense. In 1894, the church was struck by lightning, the tower being much damaged, the clock destroyed, and the bells partly melted and broken. The fabric was subsequently restored and the bells recast and rehung, the organ repaired and enlarged, and a new clock supplied, at a cost of about £1,500. In 1906 an oak chancel screen was erected. The church once provided 250 sittings and the register dates from 1653.

Ranskill Road, Mattersey, looking to the junction leading to Mattersey Thorpe. The Blacksmith's Arms public house is on the right where, at this time, W. Ford was the landlord

Main Street, Mattersey looking towards Abbey Road with the Barley Mow Inn on the left. Lord St Oswald and Lord Middleton are listed amongst the former lords of the manor.

Street scene at Mattersey.

Members of Wiseton cricket team pose for the camera.

Dairy Cottage, Wiseton. The village largely contains eighteenth and nineteenth-century dwellings.

Wiseton is one mile north-west of Clayworth. At one time, Wisteon Hall was occupied by Lt-Col Joseph Frederick Laycock DSO, JP who was the sole landowner in the village.

Wiseton Football Club pictured in 1907.

In the gardens at Wiseton Hall. The building dated from 1771 and was occupied during the late eighteenth century by a Mr Acklam. The hall survived until 1960.

Wiseton Home Farm dairy.

The poultry yard at Wiseton Home Farm.

Wiseton post office. A former sub-postmistress was Mrs Hannah M. Corless. Letters through Bawtry arrived at 7.45 a.m. and 6.15 a.m. (callers only). The letter box was cleared at 8.55 a.m. and 6.10 p.m. There were no deliveries on Sundays.

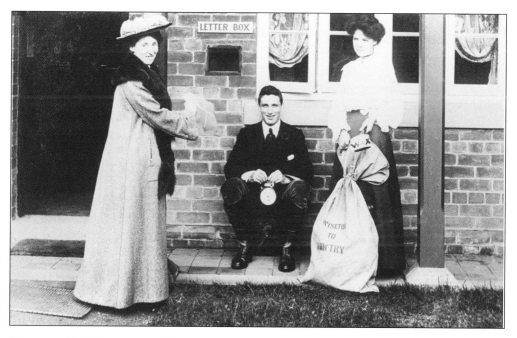

Scene outside Wiseton post office.

Wiseton stables, which survived after the hall was demolished. The buildings date from the late eighteenth century.

Street scene at Wiseton.

German prisoners renovating Wiseton cricket field. Wiseton Hall is in the background.

Wiseton motor garage.

Nottinghamshire Royal Horse Artillery at Wiseton, before the First World War. The group was formed by Brigadier General Sir Joseph Laycock.

Primrose League fête at Wiseton.

Rose garden at Wiseton.

Clayworth is on the old Roman road stretching from Lincoln to Doncaster and adjacent to the old Chesterfield canal, six miles north of East Retford. The Brewer's Arms public house is on the left.

A street scene at Clayworth. The principal landowners in the area at the turn of the nineteenth century were Broomhead Collins Fox Esq. and Robert Charles Otter.

Royston Manor, the south front allegedly dating from around 1588. However, much of what can be seen was rebuilt in 1891. For a long period the house was occupied by the Otter family.

Street scene at Clayworth.

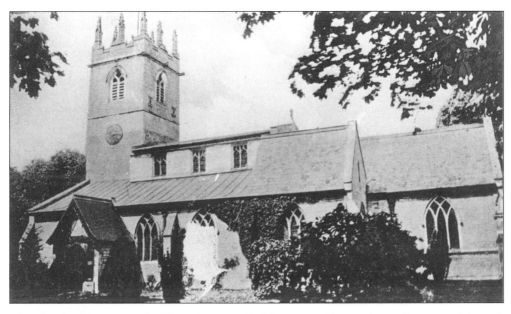

The church of St Peter is a building of stone in the Norman and later styles, and consists of chancel, separated from the nave by a handsome oak screen, nave, aisles, south porch and an embattled tower at the west end with eight pinnacles. The north aisle extends to the whole length of the chancel and the south aisle is prolonged by a chapel, named after St Nicholas. An arcade of two bays separates the aisles from the nave, which is lighted by a clerestory pierced with three Perpendicular windows on each side. The whole fabric was restored, a new font erected and the interior fitted with open benches in 1874-75 under the direction of Sir G. Gilbert Scott RA and re-opened in June 1875 at a cost of £3,459 of which £1,000 was contributed by a late rector. The parish register dates from 1545.

The chancel of Clayworth church, which is decorated by murals painted by Scottish artist Phoebe Traquir in 1905.

The Clayworth village football team of 1908.

Rectors outing, Clayworth, 1912. The picture was taken by P. Bradbury of Gainsborough.

The Hall, Clayworth, situated just south of the church is a plain and much-altered late eighteenth or early nineteenth-century stuccoed house. Listed amongst its occupants was James Percy Marshall.

A street scene at Clayworth with the Blacksmith's public house on the left. At the outset of the twentieth century, the occupations in the village were largely related to agriculture and included a farmer, fruit grower, market gardener, shop keeper, wood carver, a blacksmith and a fruit grower.

Looking along Town Street at Clayworth with the Brewer's Arms public house on the right. Katy's cottage and the road to Misterton and Gringley are just beyond the premises. One of the pub's licensees was John Broom.

The scene just a little closer than the last, featuring Lea cottage on the left.

Town Street, Clayworth, looking towards Church Lane. Clayworth is situated on the old Roman road from Lincoln to Doncaster.

Town Street, Clayworth, with St Peter's Lane to the left.

Canal bridge at Clayworth. At the outset of the twentieth century, the area was a village, township and parish, on the Chesterfield canal, four miles north-west from Sturton station on the Sheffield and Cleethorpes section of the Great Central railway, six south-east from Bawtry, six north from East Retford and eight west from Gainsborough.

Ten

Around Beckingham and Gringley

The post office at Beckingham. Beckingham is a parish and large village nine miles north-east of Retford. Around this time George Herbert N. Bee was the sub-postmaster.

Gringley-on-the-Hill is eight miles north of East Retford. In this view of the High Street looking north, the White Hart and Blue Bell public houses are on the right.

Another view of the High Street. At one time, the Duke of Portland was lord of the manor of Gringley.

Village scene at Gringley-on-the-Hill.

Horsewells, Gringley-on-the-Hill. Most of the properties on the left of the picture had been cleared by the start of the Second World War.

Above and below: Two views showing Gringley Boy Scouts posing for the camera.

Gringley bonfire. Taken during the Coronation celebrations at Gringley.

Above and below: Convalescent home for children at Gringley Hall. It was once stated that the chief advantage of Gringley-on-the-Hill is its beautiful situation. 'It is a good resort as a sanatorium, being high and dry in winter and bracing in summer.' (*Kelly's Directory*, 1911)

A village scene at Gringley. A former lord of the manor and principal landowner was Lt-Col J.F. Laycock. The population during the first quarter of the twentieth century was around 750.

A school group at Gringley, early twentieth century.

Above and below: Two Coronation Day scenes at Gringley.

Coronation Day scene at Gringley.

High Street facing south with the Blue Bell and White Hart public houses in the distance. The churchyard is to the right and the old vicarage is hidden by the trees.

West Wells Lane with the Primitive Methodist chapel on the right. The building carries an 1838 date stone and has since been converted to a private dwelling.

Finkell Street facing south west where the church may be seen in the distance without its pinnacle. Much redevelopment has taken place in this area during the intervening years. For many years the Gringley population was chiefly agricultural.

Gringley National schools. A public elementary school (mixed and infants) was erected on a site given by the Duke of Portland in 1855, for 100 children. A Mrs Ellen Hunt was one of the school mistresses.

Gringley church of SS Peter and Paul stands on an elevated site, and is an ancient building of stone, in the Transition and Early English styles, consisting of chancel, nave, north aisle and an embattled western tower, with four pinnacles, containing four bells. The church was restored and enlarged in 1912 at a cost of about £3,100. The work included the erection of a new south aisle and clergy vestry. The parish register dates from about 1600, and among the records is a parchment showing the subscriptions collected in this parish towards the rebuilding of St Paul's in London, after the Great Fire in 1666. Near the church is an ancient cross, with a niche towards the east.

The Green, Gringley.

Gringley burial ground and mill. The latter still survives today, albeit in a ruinous state. The cemetery is administered by the Parish Council and was opened in 1907 following the closure of the churchyard.

Misterton Hospital Saturday procession 19 June 1909.

West Stockwith Charity Band. At one time villagers were principally employed at Morris's chemical works.

North Wheatley, often described as a pleasant parish and village, is five miles north-east from East Retford. At one time Lord Middleton was lord of the manor and the principal landowner. The picture shows the Sun Inn, formerly selling Hewitt's ales. At the time the picture was taken the village population was around 400.

West Stockwith is thirteen miles north-east of East Retford. The picture here shows a scene from the hospital demonstration at West Stockwith on 2 July 1910. The population in 1911 was 666. The trade was mostly connected with shipping on the river and Chesterfield canal, the parish being on the tideway. Pevsner *op. cit* describes it as a 'riverside village all of brick, almost as if it were in Holland (It was an inland port with a barge basin and warehouses at the junction of the rivers Idle and Trent and the Chesterfield Canal, opened in 1775). The Church fits perfectly into this picture.'